The Financial Advisor's Estate Planning Desk Reference

How to deepen your relationships with your clients, provide even better service to them, and increase their whole family's loyalty towards you

Daniel E. McKenzie, Esq.

ISBN: 978-1-6847-0585-6 (sc)
ISBN: 978-1-6847-0584-9 (e)

Lulu Publishing Services rev. date: 06/26/2019

Contents

Acknowledgments

I have never written a book before, probably because the idea of doing so seemed overwhelming. And the last thing it seemed I needed was an overwhelming task. Starting a law firm after 10 years of being someone else's associate, in an area of law in which I had not specialized, has been the most challenging task I have ever taken on. Those who have started their own businesses know that the burdens associated with that do not fall on the would-be businessperson alone. All of those in their lives, including both family and co-workers, get to ride that wave with them, whether they want to or not. So thank you to everyone in those categories who has had to deal with a person who was, on occasion, just this side of sane.

My wife, especially, has been close to this, not only because she is my wife, but she is also my paralegal, co-office manager, blogger, and general problem solver. She also copy-edited this book. All of that in addition to handling the day-to-day management of raising our four kids. It is more than most could handle. Yet somehow, between the two of us, she has been the more even keeled and able to stay rational about what both the business and our family need to focus on next.

Also, a special acknowledgment to my parents and in laws. I frequently joke that if I had actually done the planning I should have done before deciding to leave the comforts of employment, I would not have done it. The cliché about entrepreneurs building the airplane after jumping off the cliff is a more accurate metaphor for what I did than I wish to admit. I would love to report that the only reason we have played this long is because of my heroic decision-making abilities, but the reality is that I would not have lasted a year if it had not been for some key substantial financial support from all of them.

Thank you everyone.

Introduction

Many of my interactions with financial professionals have included the following conversations: Should you care whether your clients plan their estates? If so, why? Is estate planning an urgent problem that everyone needs to address immediately, or that can be put off until clients have reached a certain age? Or a certain level of wealth? Or who have health issues? Are there other financial goals your clients should achieve before spending money on estate planning?

Once you have decided to encourage a client to get an estate plan, how do you direct them? Do they need a lawyer's help or is a fill-in-the-blanks solution sufficient? Is a bad plan better than no plan? How do you help your clients distinguish a good plan from a bad plan? How much should it cost?

I have written this book to help wealth planning and risk management professionals:

1. Understand what estate planning is, how it works, and what it can accomplish.
2. Determine how to help clients accomplish this important task.
3. Use the estate planning process to deepen their relationship with their clients and increase their clients' loyalty towards them.

All professional service providers are under more pressure than ever to prove their value to a skeptical public. We know the value we bring to our clients, the years of training we have undergone and continue to pursue, the heartbreaking stories we hear of people who failed to plan, etc. As consumers, we are all benefiting from a seismic shift in the availability of information, but as service providers, whose product is knowledge, there has never been a more challenging time to be in business.

I remember going to car lots with my dad when I was a kid. He was a voracious researcher when it came to large purchases, and a formally trained business negotiator. Back then, he operated on a fraction of the information we currently have in our pockets. Before the advent of the internet, there was simply no easy way to find out what the dealership paid for the car, price the same car at different dealerships, or compare what other consumers recently bought it for. Walking into a dealership without that information meant that my dad had to rely on his wits and understanding of transactional psychology to get the best deal. Like many others of his generation, my dad preferred to form a relationship with one salesman or dealership where he knew he would receive personal attention and reasonable prices, even if it meant he did not find the absolute lowest price on the car he wanted.

Today, it is almost unimaginable that a consumer would be willing to pay slightly more for a car if they knew they could get it for $100 cheaper at the dealership 50 miles away (the last car I bought was brought in from the next state over by an auto broker). Walking into a dealership at all is becoming an increasingly antiquated thing to do. Developing personal relationships with sales professionals is even more rare. Even the purchase of major consumer goods is being commoditized. Increasingly, clients are being trained not to trust.

What happens to professionals who tout themselves as a "trusted advisor" in a world where trust is harder to earn than ever before?

Consumers are also being encouraged to believe that they can do it themselves, whatever "it" may be. Or maybe, not by themselves, exactly, but with the help of an algorithm. Who needs a lawyer when you can just fill out a form on the internet? Who needs a banker when you can supposedly set your own loan terms on your phone? Even jobs that would seem to require a trained, licensed, and insured professional are being amateurized (or, depending on your point of view, democratized). We are all one app download away from becoming professional taxi drivers. A task that used to be a respectable job that required significant investment in expensive licensing has now been relegated (or, again depending on your point of view, opened up) to a "side hustle."

You might think that this do-it-yourself revolution and the "gig economy" would not affect those of us who have spent tens of thousands (sometimes more) of dollars on specialized education and hours more getting the licenses needed to ply our trades. Surely there are certain professions that are so complex and specialized that no one would consider going without professional help. Alas, no. In fact, in some ways, the complexity of what we do works against us. You may have heard of the Dunn-Krueger effect, the situation in which a person's ignorance about the complexity of a certain subject actually increases their confidence about their ability, because they *do not know what they do not know*. People are almost pathologically unwilling to consider the possibility that their circumstances are more complicated than they might realize. I bet if you survey your clients and ask them whether they need more than a simple will, the vast majority will scoff. After all, their families get along. They do not have any exotic investments. But as you will see in this book, a "simple will" (a term that, itself, may have more nuance than most people realize) is *rarely* appropriate.

So what can we do? The answer, I suggest, is to find ways to provide service that no algorithm can possibly provide. An algorithm can create a stock portfolio. It can take your family's names and insert them into a template document. But an algorithm can only answer questions that you ask it. Algorithms cannot proactively find problems you did not realize you had and connect you to solutions. Your ability to discern potential issues and connect your clients to a team of people who can integrate truly individualized solutions is a differentiator that no server or offshore solution will be able to match.

This book contains one suggestion as to how you might pursue this in your chosen profession.

Chapter 1
Estate Planning: More than you think it is

If you are an adult with any assets at all, you have an estate plan.

So what is estate planning? You may think the answer is obvious, but I bet if you ask your clients, a significant number will struggle to come up with anything more than a vague definition. Those that do will likely equate estate planning with a Will – a written statement of who should get their stuff when they die. It is no wonder that so many people fail to prioritize estate planning when they have such a limited view of what it is.

A point that I frequently make to my clients is that if you are an adult with any assets at all, you have an estate plan. Whether you have done your planning deliberately or cohesively is another matter. Are you married? Marriage is, among other things (hopefully), an estate planning decision. Did you buy property jointly with your spouse, girlfriend, child, or business partner? Estate planning. Have you bought life insurance? Estate planning. Did you designate the person who would receive your 401(k) if it still has money in it at the time of your death? Estate planning. Have you ever received a significant gift or loan from your parents (or given one to your kids) to buy a house, start a business, or contribute to your kid's college fund? Estate planning. Have you ever designated an emergency contact with a medical provider? Estate planning. Most people have probably done at least one thing on this list by the time they are 30, if not all of them.

And so the problem is not so much that your clients do not have an estate plan. It is that they are putting that plan together in pieces and chunks, at different times of their lives, with little to no thought, whenever an insurance or HR professional sticks a form in front of them. They are planning without a cohesive goal or philosophy. At best, this scattershot approach will probably be extremely difficult for their surviving family members to figure out, especially during an emergency. At worst, it will lead to people inadvertently being cut out of the plan, being given more money than they are ready to handle, substantial time in court getting the necessary authority to proceed on the deceased's behalf, etc., etc., etc.

Moreover, most people fail to fully think through every situation that can arise in which you would need someone to pay your bills, talk to your doctors, take care of your kids, etc. As noted above, most of your clients likely equate estate planning with providing instructions on who gets what when you die. That is certainly part of it, but only part, and maybe not the most important part. In fact, in addition to post-death asset distribution, a comprehensive estate plan covers, among other topics:

1. Disability planning
2. Guardians for minor kids
3. Money management for beneficiaries
4. Asset protection
5. Tax planning
6. Naming the right people to the right jobs

Not just your documents

While people often underestimate the importance of having a will, they frequently overestimate what a will accomplishes. Many people think if they have a will, they have an estate plan. Sorry. Not even close. In fact, in many cases, a will does not do anything. Yes, you read that right: in many cases, a will does not do anything. That is because a will only controls property that you own by yourself at the time of your death, and which does not have any beneficiary instruction attached to it.

Usually, that means that, when one member of a married couple dies, his or her will never even gets taken off the shelf. The surviving spouse frequently gets everything, either as the joint owner of all the assets or as their designated beneficiary. The order in which property is distributed is as follows:

1. **Lifetime gifts**. You may not think of giving away gifts as estate planning, but back when the total amount you could give away before estate tax became due was only in the hundreds of thousands of dollars, lifetime transfers of assets was a frequently used strategy to shrink estates below the tax threshold. Now that the estate tax threshold is so high ($11.2 million for a single person, or $22.4 million for a married couple at the time of this writing), this is a much less frequently used strategy. Especially since gifts received during lifetime come with the gifter's capital gains basis, whereas gifts received after death come with a stepped up basis, a potentially massive tax swing that should not be overlooked. There are, of course, still reasons for family members to exchange gifts, despite potentially negative tax consequences, including equalization of gifts provided to siblings and protection of assets in seconds marriages.

2. **Jointly held property**. When someone dies, any property or accounts they held jointly with someone who is still alive goes to that living person. But there are a couple of landmines to watch out for here.

   First, there is more than one way to hold property together with someone else, and if you mean for the survivor to automatically take ownership of the whole thing when one owner dies, you need to be sure you have said so. If you do not explicitly specify survivorship rights, you may own the property as tenants in common, meaning you each own a proportional share of the property separately. This may further mean that one day, you will co-own your house with your spouse's kids. Fine, *if that's what you mean to do*. If not, it is frequently a disaster. Many couples in second marriages do mean for their half of the property to go to their descendants, and not their spouse.

Second, a lot of older people put their adult kids on their houses and bank accounts with the thought that doing so will enable their kids to help with lifetime financial management, and then receive those assets quickly and easily without the need for probate after death. It does accomplish both those things, but it also opens up your assets to attack by your kids' creditors, saddles them with your capital gains basis, and can trigger the need to file a gift tax return. Moreover, if only one kid of several was added to the ownership, other kids may feel slighted when the kid who was added during lifetime gets the whole thing. Maybe the intention was for them to share, but the kid who was put on that account has no legal obligation to share it with anyone. And doing so may again trigger issues with capital gains taxes and gift tax returns.

3. **Designated beneficiary instructions**. Designated beneficiary instructions can be a godsend or a disaster. They rarely seem to fall anywhere in between. What many people fail to realize is that their designated beneficiary instructions supersede their wills, regardless of which one was done first. This can be fabulous! One of the benefits of life insurance, for example, is that it gets cash to those who need it quickly, without the need to wait for a probate to even be initiated, let alone finished. But too many times, people forget how long it has been since they filled out those instructions, or how much has changed since they did so. Or they think their more recently executed will updates everything. For better or worse, it does not, and conflicting or outdated instructions can lead to unintended results that are almost impossible to undo.

4. **Entities**. Entities such as LLCs and trusts can offer both an effective and efficient way to pass assets, because unlike people, entities do not die or suffer disabilities. Keep in mind, however, that entities can only control the assets that are titled to them. So many people think they are done planning when they sign their trust agreements, but funding the trust (and keeping it funded as assets continue to be bought and sold) is just as important as creating the trust in the first place.

The funding process may present the best opportunity for you as the financial advisor to provide a value-added service for the client and learn more about their assets (including assets not under your custodianship), as well as their long-term goals and concerns. Most financial advisors ask their clients, at least during the initial intake, whether they have an estate plan. When your clients say yes, you should then ask them whether that plan is funded and properly coordinated with their titling and beneficiary designations. A significant majority of them will ask you what you mean, a major opportunity for you to shine.

5. **Will.** A client's will only controls what remains after property has been distributed by any of the mechanisms mentioned above. For married couples especially, this means that if one member of the couple dies before the other, that first-to-die's will often does not end up directing anything. Frequently, all the property goes to the survivor via joint ownership and designated beneficiary instructions, and that survivor ultimately gets to decide where things go. A lot of married couples assume that this is what they want, but there are at least a couple of potential problems to keep in mind.

     First, if the first-to-die had kids separately from the survivor, this might result in those kids never getting anything from their decreased parent's estate. The couple might assume, and promise to each other, that they will keep each other's kids in their respective plans. But there is nothing legally binding about such a promise, and in my experience, people tend to overestimate how closely they will stay in touch with their step-kids after those kids' parent is no longer around. Even clients in their 70s can outlive each other by decades, a long time to maintain a relationship with someone after your only connection to them is no longer around.

     You may think this problem could not arise in situations where there are no step kids. Step kids, however, always could be acquired in the future even by people who are happily in their first marriages. It is, of course, common for widows and widowers to remarry, even when their widowhood came late in life. If you have kids, and want to be sure those kids are the ultimate beneficiaries of your estate, you probably need to put your significant assets in a trust, rather than handing them directly to your spouse.

Your spouse can be the beneficiary of that trust during his or her lifetime (or until he or she gets remarried), with your kids designated as the recipients of anything that remains.

6. **State law.** Any property still in the decedent's name at this point gets distributed according to state law. This is not necessarily awful. A lot of people assume this would result in the government receiving their property. Probably not. While it varies from state to state, each state's rules about what happens to property not directed by one of the mechanisms above do try to mimic what most people want: *i.e.*, everything to the surviving spouse and then equally to the kids. But within that vanilla plan, lots of potential disasters lurk.

Among the unanswered questions are the following. If there are minor kids, who will take care of them and who will take care of their money? What happens if those kids are not emotionally ready to receive whatever money is left when they reach 21? Who gets to make the decisions about how the assets in the estate will be split up, liquidated, and passed to those legally entitled to receive them? These questions, and many more, can be the source of a lot of confusion, fighting, and unnecessary expense.

Chapter 2
What is probate?

Hanging over the decision about which mechanisms to rely on to get your stuff where you want it to go is the probate process. There are lots of common misunderstandings about probate, starting with what, exactly, it is.

If you die with assets titled in your name, someone is going to need to take control of those assets and hand them over to the people legally entitled to receive them. But you can't just walk into the county clerk's office, or a bank, or the DMV, or the 401(k) custodian's branch office and walk out of there with the money, or the title, or the deed, even if you are a close family member. If you try, you can expect to be asked, "How do we know that the owner of this asset is dead? Who are you? How do we know who is legally entitled to receive this asset? How do we know if we give this thing to you that you will give it to the people legally entitled to receive it? How do we know there is not anyone out there to whom this person owed money?" The probate court is there to answer those questions and ensure that the law gets followed.

When does probate happen?

Probate does not have to be done for everyone. We do not want to clog up the courts administering estates that have only a few assets in them. To ensure that it is worthwhile, each state has a minimum amount of assets that need to be present before a probate *has* to be opened (there can be situations where a probate ends up needing to be opened even when this threshold is not met, such as when there are significant creditor claims that need to be resolved). If the decedent had less than that minimum, one of the beneficiaries can usually take a "small estate affidavit" to any person or entity in possession of any asset of the decedent's. In the affidavit, the signer swears under oath that: (1) the decedent did not have enough assets to require probate; and (2) that he or she will distribute the asset to the people entitled to receive it (note that a small estate affidavit does not give the person who is being given the asset the right to keep it unless he or she is legally entitled to do so as a beneficiary and the other beneficiaries receive their fair shares).

The probate process

The probate process serves a number of purposes. The overarching purpose is to ensure that the people entitled to receive a decedent's assets get them. That does not just mean the person's family members, or those that the decedent named in a will. Anyone to whom the decedent owed money also has a right to at least submit a request for repayment. To accomplish this goal, the following process is utilized:[1]

1. **Application.** Somebody who is interested in having the estate administered (probably because they anticipate they are entitled to receive something from it) submits an application to open a probate to the probate court for the county in which the decedent was residing at the time of death. The application includes information about the decedent, such as where he or she was living at the end of his or her life, the date he or she died, whether he or she had a will and if so, when that will was executed, the relationship of the person submitting the application to the decedent, and a list of the decedent's heirs (*i.e.,* the people who would be entitled to inherit under state law if there was no will). A copy of the application

---

[1] Again, this description is based on Colorado law. Most states follow a similar chronology of tasks and events, but there can be significant variety. And so if you are advising people who own property in started besides Colorado, you should advise them to speak with an attorney well versed in that state's laws.

needs to be sent to all of the heirs so that they can object to the applicant's appointment or submit their own applications.

Typically, the application is evaluated by the court clerk, and if it appears to contain all the required content and no objections have been received, the clerk will issue a document called "letters" to the applicant, which is the document that officially transforms the applicant into the personal representative of the estate. The personal representative uses those letters to collect the decedent's assets and re-title them to the estate for later distribution.

2. **Notify heirs**. Once the estate has been opened, the heirs need to be notified that the probate has been opened, which court is overseeing it, who the personal representative is, and where to submit complaints or requests for information. Note that this notification requirement is not just for people who appear to be entitled to receive something from the estate, but for anyone who would have been entitled to a distribution under state law. That means that even if there is a will that disinherits someone, that person needs to be notified so that they can challenge the validity of that will in court.

3. **Inventory**. After getting the needed authority from the court, the personal representative then needs to create an inventory of the assets being probated. This is not necessarily every asset the decedent had, only those assets that need to be distributed through the probate process – i.e., assets that were not distributed through joint ownership, designated beneficiary instructions, or a trust or other entity. The personal representative also needs to figure out how much debt the decedent had, and to whom it was owed.

4. **Notify creditors**. While most people are focused on getting assets to the decedent's beneficiaries, perhaps the most important part of the probate process, at least to the personal representative, is ensuring that the decedent's creditors are properly notified. If they are not, and the assets get distributed, and then a creditor who was not properly notified shows up, the personal representative can be personally on the hook for the amount due if he or she cannot claw back the assets from the people who received them.

There are two different processes for notifying creditors. The first is to publish a newspaper ad, letting potential creditors know that the decedent has died, that a probate has been opened, and the deadline for letting the personal representative know that you were owed money. The other way to notify creditors is to send a notice directly to the creditors, something that the personal representative must do for creditors he or she knows about or should know about. Both need to be done if the personal representative wants to close the probate in less than a year and wants to be absolutely sure no new creditor claims can be asserted.

5. **Administration.** This is often the most challenging part of the probate for the personal representative and the point at which fighting between the beneficiaries is most likely to occur. This is the point at which the personal representative carries out the distribution plan. This can be more difficult than most people realize.

Let us say the plan says to split everything equally between the decedent's three adult kids, probably the most common instruction given. Sounds pretty uncontroversial, right?

First, imagine having to divide your own stuff into three equal piles. How easy would that be? How much is your 10 year old furniture, décor, or TV worth? How do you deal with items that have no market value, but which may have substantial sentimental value? Along those lines, how do you deal with petty or vindictive family members who claim deep attachment to certain items just to irritate other family members or gain leverage over family members who really do care about them? Is the goal to maximize the value of the estate or to get it distributed quickly? Should we sell the home or rent it out? Use a real estate agent or sell it ourselves? Fix it up first or sell it to a flipper? There are more questions like these in the typical probate process than I could possibly recount.

The difficulty of these questions are compounded if, as frequently is the case, the personal representative is also one of the beneficiaries. In that situation, that person is inherently conflicted and ripe to have their motives questioned by people who want to make his or her life difficult.

Other situations that can further complicate matters:

a. **Simmering, unresolved childhood resentments**. Many times, even the kids did not realize these were still there until those relationships are put to the test in a way they have never been tested before.

b. **Simmering, unresolved adulthood resentments**. If one of the kids was stuck taking care of declining parents at the end of life while another was living across the country, the kid who did the care-taking may not feel that an equal distribution is a fair one. On the other end of the spectrum, if one of the kids has remained more financially dependent on the decreased parents than another, the more independent kid might feel punished by an equal distribution.

c. **Substantial disparity in the financial situations of the beneficiaries**. If one of the beneficiaries truly needs the cash while another is in no hurry, a seemingly simple decision, such as whether to accept a purchase offer received for the house, can trigger thermonuclear war.

d. **Lack of liquidity.** The absence of cash ends marriages and business partnerships, usually badly. Imagine what it does to people who were forced into working together under inherently difficult circumstances instead of choosing to do so.

6. **Accounting**. Throughout the process, the personal representative needs to keep track of *every penny* coming in and going out of the estate. For example, the proceeds received from a house or estate sale result in money coming in. Money spent on hiring a contractor to repair the roof prior to sale would be money going out. Both would need to be listed on the accounting. Before closing the estate, the accounting needs to be made available to the other beneficiaries and the personal representative needs to be able to produce the receipts out other supporting documentation, if asked. Some of that documentation can be years old by this point.

7. **Wrap up**. Once the personal representative feels confident that he or she has properly addressed all creditor claims and distributed all estate assets to their rightful recipients, he or she submits the final accounting to the court, along with a signed document swearing

under oath that everything has been properly completed. Those documents get sent to the beneficiaries too.

There are two different processes to accomplish this: the formal process and the informal process. The informal process entails less court involvement than the formal process, but gives the beneficiaries much longer to object than the formal process. Beneficiaries of an estate closed with the formal process only have 30 days to object after the estate is closed, whereas beneficiaries of an informally closed estate have up to a year. The choice of which one to use depends on the personal representative's level of confidence that all potential issues have been identified and addressed to all the interested parties' satisfaction (interested parties can also ask for a formal closing if they think the court needs to conduct a closer evaluation). In certain situations, such as insolvent estates where there are more creditor claims than assets, the formal process has to be used.

The pros and cons of probate

Now that we know what probate is, the question is: should everyone try to avoid it? In Colorado, the general consensus among attorneys seems to be no, not everyone. The answer depends on a number of factors, most notably, which states you own property in. If your estate is large enough, or contains real estate, your personal representative will need to open a probate matter in every state in which you have property that needs to be collected. The variance in time and cost for what it takes to get an estate through probate in the different states is substantial.

In some states, an estate can be gotten through probate in weeks at a cost that could be described as administrative. In other states, the process takes years, requires the help of an attorney, and can cost tens of thousands of dollars. Some people hate the idea of having a court involved in their private affairs even if they are not expecting the administration of their estates to be particularly difficult or expensive. But if you are thinking that the probate process generally sounds okay, you should confirm that you do not own property in one of those more difficult states before settling on a planning strategy.

Assuming that you only own property in states that have reasonable probate processes, there are still a couple of reasons people do not like probate. First, it is public. In the United States, the default rule is that court proceedings are open to the public unless a compelling argument is made as to why they should not be (*i.e.,* trade secrets may be revealed or sensitive sexual matters may be discussed). You may think that you are hardly well known enough to warrant public scrutiny, but in fact, the county clerks do sell lists of all the probate cases, along with contact information for each estate's personal representative. Your personal representative can count on being contacted by real estate agents and other solicitors looking to sell goods and services to the survivors of the recently decreased. It can at least be annoying, if not occasionally sinister.

Second, yes, it is a court proceeding. As a lawyer and a former litigator, I have substantial respect for our judicial system. But whatever strengths that system has, speed and predictability are not usually among them. Most probates go as expected. But once you introduce an outside party to the proceedings and start forcing notifications to be sent to everyone who conceivably has an in interest in the proceedings, there is no telling what issues might pop up. Especially when that outside party is a cold blooded, underfunded, understaffed bureaucracy that does not necessarily aspire to winning customer service awards.

Third, because a probate matter is an open court case, it is easy for people who want to make things difficult to do so. If you have a potentially problematic family member, the requirement that certain information be disclosed to heirs (or even to anyone who has registered an interest with the court), easy access to a court into which they can lodge complaints can throw a lot of sand in the gears and can make things difficult. This relates back to the privacy issue. If you have an heir that you think might be unhappy with your plan, you should strongly consider whether forcing your estate's representative to run its administration through a public process is a good idea (on the other hand, having a judge available to help manage a difficult situation can be a positive).

Is a "simple will" good enough?

If you ask your clients what kind of estate plan they need, my guess is that most of them will tell you "just a simple will." But if you poke that answer just a little bit, in most cases you are going to quickly find that their claim to just need a simple will is based on: (a) not knowing what they are talking about, and (b) wanting to believe it can be done cheaply. We have already seen how little your will can end up controlling (nothing, in many situations). A will is only part of your estate plan, and the number of extremely common situations that take you out of "simple" territory, such as having a kid or entering a second marriage, are high.

What is a simple will?

Before getting into a debate about whether a simple will is good enough, we need to determine what makes a will simple. Most people assume that a shorter document is simpler than a longer one. A 2 page will must be simpler than a 20 page will, right? The fallacy behind this logic can be exposed by taking it to its logical extreme. If size is all that matters, then the simplest plan is no plan at all, right? As I frequently tell my clients, if short and cheap is your only goal, take that napkin in front of you, write "everything to my spouse, if she survives me, then everything to my kids in equal shares," sign it, and you can now say that, yes, you have a simple will.

But let's take a step back for a moment. When you say "simple will," simple for who? Remember that a will involves three parties: the person who drafts it, the person who has to administer it, and the person who will receive the goodies that it will distribute (note that latter two positions could be held by one person or multiple people each, or some combination of the two). What is easy for one of those parties might be hard for the others.

Let's go back to our napkin example to see why. Yes, it is short. It would not take you even two minutes to write it, and even less time to read it. But if you are the one who has to implement those instructions, what would you expect to be easier? Vague, short, incomplete instructions or highly detailed instructions that cover everything? Yes, that highly detailed, comprehensive will may seem like overkill, but which would you rather have to try to figure out: a will that contains some provisions that are not applicable or a will that is missing instructions that are badly needed? You can skip over instructions that are not relevant. Having to fill in gaps, on the other hand, raises the likelihood that professional legal help, and maybe even a court, will need to get involved.

Obviously, this does not mean that longer wills are simpler than shorter ones. But they can be, and your clients should definitely not assume that a short will is either adequate or better than a long will.

What about no plan? Is any plan always better than no plan? Well, first of all, I would say that choosing not to plan is a plan. And as explained earlier, whether or not you have a will, if you own something with someone else or have completed a designated beneficiary instruction, you have engaged in estate planning.

But most people do not realize that, and one thing I frequently hear from potential clients is, "We just want to get something simple in place for now, and we'll get a real plan in place when…" take your pick: when we have our baby; when we're done having kids; when our youngest kid turns 18. Etc., etc., etc.

But the answer to the question about whether having a will is always better than not having a will, the answer is an absolute, definite, unmitigated NO! You absolutely can make things worse with a poorly thought out, incomplete document, or a document that names the wrong people to fill the various positions that need to be filled in even a basic estate plan, and can end up causing so much more pain and heartache than just having a court figure it out using state law.

Situations that are common, but not simple

One reason so many people think that all they need is a simple will is because they do not see anything unusual about their family or financial situations.

But there are many common situations that cannot be adequately dealt with by a will alone. "Common" and "simple" are two different things that people constantly mistakenly conflate with one another. Let's consider a few situations that are common but not necessarily simple:

1. **Minor kids.** Yup. Just having a kid (probably the most common reason why people do estate planning in the first place) takes you out of "simple will" territory. The presence of minors raises two issues that need to be addressed.

   First, money cannot be given directly to kids. If your will or your designated beneficiary instructions name kids as your beneficiaries, a court is going to have to appoint someone to manage that money for them until they reach adulthood. This person is called the "conservator." Not only does the court have to appoint the conservator, but it has to keep monitoring that person's efforts on your kids' behalf. Your children's conservator will at least have to file accounting reports with the court every year, if not submit to constant supervision of your child's money via a "restricted account" that can only be accessed with court permission.

   Perhaps more importantly, if you did not leave any instructions as to who should manage your kids' money, you probably did not leave any instructions as to how that money should be managed either. And even if you did, the second issue is that the conservator's authority ends, and the money becomes your kids', to do with as they please, when they turn 21. Windfalls are rarely handled well, even by people who have been responsible adults for decades. What chance do your kids have of figuring this out before they have graduated from college?

   If you have minor kids, your plan must include a trust to avoid this situation. The trust holds your kids' assets for them under the management of a trustee. You get to choose the trustee. You get to provide the guidance and instructions so that the trustee knows when to make distributions for or to the child. You get to determine when, if ever, the child gets to take unrestricted control of the money.

2. **Adult kids not ready to receive a windfall.** Whatever their wealth, I bet if asked, most of your clients would be reluctant to describe themselves as "wealthy." Many of them would likely be skeptical that they have an amount of wealth that could potentially be ruinous. But as I always point out to my clients, a vast majority of your wealth may be tied up in ways that make it extremely difficult for you to access. Home equity, life insurance death benefits, and tax deferred retirement accounts can easily add up to hundreds of thousands, if not millions of dollars, even for people who feel like they struggle to save. But their children would have unimpeded access to every single one of those dollars if they were to inherit those assets.

   Now, your clients may be thinking, "Okay, that's true, but my kids are fine. They wouldn't do anything dumb with it." The statistics, however, on what usually gets done with windfalls indicate otherwise. A huge majority of the time, no matter how much is received, sudden unearned wealth gets spent quickly, on frivolous items. Even if it does not go to heroin and hookers, the most responsible people find it hard not to think of an inheritance as "found money" that can be frittered away on things like fancier vacations, nicer cars, and home remodels. Maybe it is not a total disaster, but it certainly is a missed opportunity.

3. **Predators and creditors.** Even if your kids are responsible and unlikely to quickly spend the money like the vast majority of people do, there can frequently be situations beyond their control that can cause the newfound wealth to disappear quickly.

   Now again, your clients may be thinking, "My kids aren't the type to get into trouble with debt." There are a lot of ways, however, to pick up creditors beyond irresponsible spending. A divorce, the development of an expensive medical problem, a contentious breakup with a business partner, a lawsuit (people in some of the most high paying, but also high liability, professions, such as medicine or law, should probably never be given their inheritance outright), can all result in a financially ruinous level of debt for someone through no fault of their own. In these situations, receiving an outright distribution from a simple will can, again, be an enormous lost opportunity as the money goes right through your kid's hands to... who? A daughter-in-law you never liked?

4. **Step kids**. If you have kids from a relationship prior to your current marriage, or if your spouse does, you both need to think carefully through how you want to support each other, and then your kids. The most often committed oversight people with step kids make is to leave their estates outright to each other without any thought as to what will happen to those assets after the second spouse passes away. You may have some sort of agreement with each other that the second to die will leave half of his or her estate to the other's kids. You may have even executed wills together that say that. But relationships fade and wills can be changed. Even if you are in your seventies, your partner could still outlive you by decades, or vice versa. One of you could still get remarried (an event that *will* change your estate plan unless you proactively plan to prevent it)! The odds of at least one of those things happening is higher than you think. You and your spouse may have the best of intentions, but as always, unforeseen events can result in unforeseen outcomes.

5. **Special needs child**. Children who have needs that might qualify them for government assistance, such as Social Security Disability Income or Medicaid, should never be given money outright because doing so might disqualify them from receiving those benefits while not providing them with enough funds to cover all their needs. Some people address this problem by completely disinheriting their special needs kid. That is like quitting your job to avoid paying taxes. It solves one problem, but can create a much bigger one. A better solution is to create a special needs trust, the funds from which can only be used to cover items that government benefits do not cover. These types of trusts require especially careful drafting to ensure they comply with the very complex requirements of the various government programs for which someone with special needs could potentially qualify.

6. **Significant retirement assets.** For many people, retirement assets comprise either their first or second most valuable asset, with only the house comprising a larger share. Significant tax

deferred savings present an enormous opportunity for people with just modest overall wealth to pass along a gift that could stretch past more than one generation. The reason is that, although a person who inherits an IRA or 401(k) is required to begin taking distributions, regardless of their age, if they have the discipline to leave all the remaining funds in the account, they can continue to enjoy tax free growth on that money. You can force that discipline by running the distribution of that account through a trustee. Again, many people assume their kids would not make such a financially destructive decision as to pull all the funds out, lose the tax deferral, and pay income taxes on it. But again, the statistics indicate that people do not mind paying taxes on "found money." Even with the tax hit, it is more money than they had before. Few people think to look at the opportunity costs, which are often substantial. Also, money that is distributed outright rather than through a trustee is not protected, either from the beneficiary's bad decisions or bad luck.

7. **Closely held businesses**. A closely held business, especially a family business, can be one of the thorniest estate planning issues. Often times in these situations, one of the kids is way more involved in the business than their siblings. The kids who are not involved may resent the kid who appears to be getting both a job and a valuable asset handed to him. The kid who is receiving the business may resent his siblings for not having to deal with the stress of keeping the family business alive. Or, if the business is given to all the kids, the stress of trying to operate an entity with partners you did not choose can be lethal to even the best relationships. In this situation, consistent, honest, and open communication is critical to making it work.

8. **Significant litigation risk or concern**. As noted above in the "Predators and Creditors" section, there are benefits available to your kids in receiving their inheritance with restrictions attached, as opposed to outright. This is especially true if your kids are in high liability professions, such as medicine, or engage in high risk hobbies, such as any activity that gets included at the X Games. Yes, receiving money in trust comes with more hassle

than receiving it outright, but that hassle protects it from creditors too. As a person who is in a high liability profession, I can tell you that I would much rather be the beneficiary of a trust than receive money outright.

9. **Property in multiple states**. Although the threshold for how much property you have to own before a probate process gets triggered at your death, ownership of real estate in your name, by yourself will require a court process to get transferred, even if it is highly leveraged or worth very little. This will need to be done in every state in which you own property. And so if you live in Colorado, but own a vacation property in Arizona, your representative will need to open a probate in Colorado and an ancillary probate in Arizona. Obviously, this can be a fairly significant expense and hassle, especially if one of the states involved has a longer than average, or more expensive than average, probate process.

10. **Family vacation property.** Even if your second property is in the same state as your primary residence, if your goal is to keep that property in the family, you need to consider a number of potential complexities. Real estate can be a difficult thing for people who are not married to each other and who have not negotiated any sort of business agreement with one another (*i.e.*, siblings) to suddenly co-own with one another. Sure, it is a family property, not necessarily a business entity, but there are still plenty of business decisions that need to be made. How do we split up the maintenance, tax, insurance, and HOA costs – equally or proportionally according to usage? How do we resolve disputes over who gets to use it when? Who gets to make decorative decisions? How do we resolve disputes over whether or not to spend money on upgrades? How do we resolve disputes over whether to rent it out or keep it empty for our own use? And on and on and on.

11. **Firearms**. Depending on the type of firearm, there may be certain steps that have to be taken before they can be transferred to someone else. If you do not care whether your guns get to any particular person, maybe you do not need to be too concerned about it. But if you do feel strongly that your guns end up with a specific person, you might want to consider putting those guns in

a trust specifically designed to ensure the proper transfer of those firearms, compliant with all applicable laws.

What does a typical plan include?

Keeping in mind that the documents discussed below are only part of your estate plan, and the other methods for passing property discussed above, such as titling property jointly and designating beneficiaries, may supersede them, the typical estate plan documents include:

1. **Will.** The will is probably the most well-known estate planning document. If you approached 50 random people on the street and asked them whether it is generally important for people to have wills, it would not surprise me if all of them said yes (it *would* surprise me if even 20 if them actually had a reasonably up to date one in place though). Most of them would even be able to give you a relatively accurate description of what one does: determines who gets my stuff when I die.

    Most people, however, actually overestimate what a will can accomplish in at least two ways. First, people assume that having a will in place allows their estates to be transferred without a probate process. Remember, though, that whether probate is necessary depends on how much of your assets are titled in your name alone and do not have beneficiary instructions attached at the time of your death. Whether or not there is a will has no bearing on that calculation. And in fact, verifying whether there is a will and, if so, whether it was validly and voluntarily executed by a person who knew what he or she was doing is one of the most important tasks that the probate court accomplishes.

    The second way in which people commonly overestimate what a will accomplishes is that they assume it supersedes any other instructions they have created and controls the distribution of everything they own. As explained above, however, a will only controls property that remains after jointly held property has been transferred to any surviving owners and after property that had a beneficiary designation attached has been distributed according to that instruction. A lot of times, when one spouse pre-deceases the other, all of that first-to-pass-away's property goes to the surviving spouse through those two methods and the will is never even taken out of the filing cabinet[2].

2. **Medical Power of Attorney.** While it is true that we will all eventually die, our biggest risk at any point in our lives is a disabling incident or disease, not a fatal one. If you pause to think about it, it is extremely rare, and notably tragic, for someone to instantly go from healthy to dead. For better or worse, most of our deaths will be preceded by a health decline, and that decline will include at least some time during which we are so hobbled that we cannot manage our affairs. And in fact, most of us will go through multiple times like this over the course of our lives, not just at the end. Maybe you fall off your bike and conk your head. Maybe you have to go through a particularly grueling chemo regimen. Maybe you get in a car accident and have to spend several months recuperating. It does not have to be permanent, or even long term. All you need is a moment in which a medical decision needs to be made that you cannot articulate for yourself.

Should we do this surgery or wait to see if the condition improves on its own? Should we try this drug, despite the possible side effects? Should you be moved to a different facility, or sent to see a specialist in a different facility (or different city, or different part of the country) despite the potential cost and risks?

You may assume a family member would just be able to step up and make these decisions for you. Don't count on it. Medical facilities are extremely nervous about running afoul of medical privacy laws and are sometimes unwilling to confirm even basic information about a person under their care, such as whether you are in the facility, if they are not certain that the person asking is legally authorized to know. Getting this legal authority on behalf of someone who does not have capacity to give it requires an extremely expensive, invasive, time consuming court process to

---

[2] Note that when someone dies in Colorado, you are supposed to lodge their will in their home county's court almost immediately, regardless of whether you think a probate is going to be necessary or not.

determine whether you really are incapacitated and also whether the person applying for the job is qualified to do it. Meanwhile, executing a POA is a relatively simple thing to do, and typically does not require a significant amount of customized drafting.

3. **General Power of Attorney.** The medical POA is obviously for appointing the person who would make medical decisions for you if you cannot do it for yourself. The general POA is to appoint the person who would complete financial tasks for you: opening your mail, paying your bills, moving money between your accounts, buying and selling assets, enforcing or performing on contracts, filing your tax returns, etc. In Colorado, you can also authorize your financial agent to entirely create or replace your estate plan for you by giving him or her the power to create trusts on your behalf, give away your assets as gifts, and change your designated beneficiaries on your insurance and investment accounts, but you have to very specifically make it clear that you mean to give your agent these extended powers.

Again, you might assume that, in a short-term emergency, family would be able to do this stuff for you. Again, that is a dangerous assumption to make, and almost certainly wrong. Like medical institutions, financial institutions are extremely paranoid about even giving out information, let alone control, to anyone they are not absolutely certain is legally authorized to make those choices. Even with a properly executed POA, financial institutions can be reluctant to deal with anyone other than the account owner because they do not have any way to know for sure that the POA with which they have been presented has not been revoked or replaced.

Still, as with the medical POA, a general POA is not usually a particularly difficult document to draft or execute, and the hassle one would need to go through in order to get authority to speak on your behalf after you have become unable to give that authority yourself is enormous. Again, it includes court hearings, criminal background checks, credit checks, and probably expert testimony about the incapacitated person's medical condition to determine whether he or she really does need this assistance. It is not unusual for it to cost thousands of dollars to get court authority, and that is if it goes smoothly. That tab can go to tens of thousands of dollars if there is any disagreement among family about who should be the one to fill this role.

4. **Living will**. Admittedly, death, destruction, and darkness overhang this whole conversation, and many people describe it as depressing to think about. But of all these documents, perhaps none is darker to ponder than the living will. Maybe that is because we all know that some day, all of us will die. But most of us probably hold out hope that our deaths will be quick and dignified, and maybe preceded by little to no suffering. The living will forces you to consider what you would want done if it does not end up going that way – if, at the end of your life, you are being kept alive, but only in the most technical sense, by machinery or other heroic medical efforts. In those situations, where doctors had concluded that recovery is not going to happen, would you want to keep receiving treatment? Yes, it is unpleasant to think about, but many of the most famous probate battles in the country's history have been about these situations, not money. And, boy, when there are fights about these issues, the emotions and moral issues intensify the battles far beyond fights about property.

5. **Memorial instructions**. Along with end-of-life issues, people often fail to appreciate the ferociousness of the fighting that can result from disagreements about how a loved one should be laid to rest. Burial or cremation? Open casket or closed? Religious ceremony or not? Do all the family members get invited? Who sits next to who? If you have not left instructions on these issues, who should make the decisions? Memorial instructions, either inside a will or as a separate, stand-alone document can help head off arguments about these decisions.

Typical add ons

While the documents listed above will work for people who do not mind probate and only want to pass items along to responsible adults with no strings attached, there are a few additional documents or clauses that usually need to be included for the "common, but not simple" scenarios described above:

1. **Appointment of guardian**. A common motivating factor for people to do their estate planning is having small kids, and perhaps the most important part of planning for the those kids is specifying who would be their guardian – *i.e.*, the person responsible for overseeing their day-to-day care. This usually gets done in the will. In some states (Colorado among them), you can also do it in its own standalone document.

    There are two benefits of doing it this way. First, the guardian appointment is the part of your plan most likely to need frequent updating. The person to whom you would leave one infant might be different than the person to whom you would leave 5 and 3 year olds. When your kids are young, you might not care if your guardian is in another state. But as your kids approach high school, location might start to trump just about every other consideration. Moreover, the people on your list will have their own changes that might make them a better or worse choice. They might move. They might get divorced. They might have more kids of their own. They might have become sick, or even have died. And so having your guardian list in its own separate document makes it easier to update just that part without having to touch everything. It also might enable you to specify who would take over in the event you were disabled, whereas a will only kicks in if you have passed away.

2. **Testamentary trust**. If you have someone in your life to whom you would need or want to make a bequest but who would benefit from having limits placed on their access to those assets (see section above on all the reasons why both you and the person receiving your assets might want that), you will likely need to have a trust somewhere in your plan. Some people, however, who definitely need or want a trust may feel as though creating a revocable living trust is overkill, usually because they do not currently have that many assets.

    This is fairly common for people who have small kids. Such people definitely need a trust because they cannot leave money directly to those kids, but maybe only have a little home equity and a modest 401(k). Rather than creating a whole separate trust agreement now, people in this situation often prefer to simply build their trust provisions into their will. What they are essentiality saying is, "If I die, create a trust."

This gives you all the benefits of a revocable trust with one major shortcoming: to get your assets into that trust so that they can be distributed to your beneficiaries, a probate process would need to be opened with your county court. Now, probate isn't necessarily terrible, but it isn't usually fast either. And before any insurance company is going to be willing to distribute death benefits, and before any bank is going to be willing to open up a bank account for the trust, they are going to wait to be sure that trust has been fully and properly established. And then the personal representative might (probably should) be reluctant to make a full, or even a significant, distribution until he or she is absolutely certain that the deadline for creditors to make claims against the estate has run. It is common for it to take well over a year for these tasks to get completed. In the meantime, your child's guardian will be operating under a fairly significant cloud of uncertainty.

3. **Revocable living trust agreement.** If you have decided that you need or want a trust and are willing to bear the extra cost and do the extra work typically associated with setting it up now, you will typically use at least a revocable living trust. I compare setting up a revocable living trust with setting up a company (without the overhead and profit-earning requirements). As long as you are alive and able, you are filling all three of that company's roles. You are the founder (*i.e.*, the settlor, grantor, or trustmaker), the CEO (*i.e.*, the trustee), and the only customer and employee (*i.e.*, the beneficiary). Why would you do this? Because when you have this company in place, you can specify, without the need for any court involvement, who can step into your shoes and run it if you cannot, for any reason, including a short-term disability.

For this to work properly, you have to "fund" the trust, meaning you have to re-title your significant assets from yourself to yourself as trustee. This is not the most intellectually challenging work, but it does take some persistence and organizational skills. It usually involves the following:

a. **Deed.** One of the most important things to title to the trust is any real estate you might have. As noted above, in Colorado (and most other, if not all other, states), transferring of real property will require a probate process if the decedent owned it by him- or herself (or if he or she owned it with someone else, but as tenants in common and not jointly with rights of survivorship). Recording a new deed, showing that the property is held by a trust, and not an individual, is usually as important as creating the trust in the first place.

b. **Assignment of personal property.** Another important, but often overlooked, part of estate planning generally, and trust funding specifically, is your personal property – *i.e.*, the "stuff" in your house. Your furniture, your jewelry, your firearms, your electronics, your clothes, your cleaning supplies, even your pets… *everything* inside your house that you can touch. Sometimes, there can be items with significant market value, but the sentiment I most often hear about this particular asset is, "No one is going to want my crap." Maybe, but it does still have to be dealt with, and even if there is not anything with significant market value, people often fail to appreciate the sentimental value that family members may attach to certain items.

Now, obviously, this stuff doesn't usually haves title, certainly not one that is recorded in any central repository. But it is still helpful to execute an "Assignment of Personal Property," that the trustee can show to anyone who asks that, yes, he or she does have the authority to distribute, or otherwise dispose of, these items. It can also be helpful towards keeping the assets that are outside the trust below the value threshold that triggers a probate.

c. **Other funding.** Other items that probably should be funded into the trust are probably paper assets. Savings accounts, investment accounts, mineral rights, stock certificates and bonds, LLC memberships and other closely held businesses, etc. For assets that have to be held by an individual, such as tax deferred retirement accounts (but see the next section about standalone retirement trusts), you *may* want to designate your trust as the beneficiary. Same thing for life insurance policies. The more you are able to put into your trust, the easier you will make it for your successor trustee to step in and seamlessly take over your financial affairs. And, of course, the less likely it becomes that any probate will be necessary.

4. **Standalone retirement trust**. One of the most overlooked, and underappreciated, estate planning opportunities that people have involves their tax deferred retirement accounts. Along with home equity, retirement savings are usually a person's most or second most valuable asset. Tax deferred retirement savings are a fabulous thing to inherit. They are typically highly liquid and very flexible, but those qualities may present their biggest drawback too. Because they are easy to access, many people who inherit tax deferred assets draw them down relatively quickly.

Now, the IRS does require a beneficiary to immediately begin taking RMDs, whatever their age. It wants to ensure that money does not get tied up in there forever, and they want the income tax that the beneficiary will have to pay as they take the money out. The 'M' in RMD stands for "minimum," and the IRS is more than happy for a beneficiary to take more than the required amount. You can force that discipline by directing that account to a trust, but it needs to be a special kind of trust because the IRS's process for calculating the RMD can be pretty complex when the trustee is told to do anything other than distribute the funds directly to the beneficiary immediately upon withdrawal. But this hassle can be well worth it for all the reasons that inherited trusts make sense, most notably, asset protection for the beneficiary.

Not so common (but potentially critical) add ons

While wills, testamentary trusts, and revocable living trusts work well for a lot of people, there are situations – unique assets, family members with unique needs, or unique tax situations – in which a more sophisticated plan will be needed.

1. **Irrevocable trusts**. While revocable trusts have many valuable benefits, tax minimization and asset protection are not among them, at least not for the person creating the trust. If that person needs those benefits, neither the IRS, the U.S. court system, nor the bankruptcy courts are going to let them have it easily. You have to give up control over those assets to have a plausible claim that they should not be used to compensate your creditors. The more, the better. And the sooner the better. If you do get sued, "I put my 20 year old son in charge of that trust yesterday" is going to sound a lot less compelling than: "That asset has been managed by a professional trustee in Nevada, inside of a limited partnership, held by a domestic asset protection trust for the last 10 years." When it comes to asset protection, it is not a yes or no answer as far as whether something would be protected or not. There is a sliding scale on which a number of variables will determine whether you can be forced to liquidate certain assets if you get a judgment entered against you.

    a. **Life insurance trust**. Life insurance trusts used to be much more common than they are today. Back when the estate tax threshold was only $600,000 per person and could not be combined by spouses, a half million dollar insurance policy combined with home equity and retirement savings could put people who definitely did not feel wealthy into estate tax territory. A good way to avoid that was to put that life insurance policy into an irrevocable trust with a third-party trustee because that would move it out of the insured's estate. That still works, but not too many people need that type of planning now that the estate tax threshold is more than $11 million per person and can be combined by married couples. It can still have asset protection benefits, but so can a number of other strategies that do not require the planning party to give up as much control as an ILIT does.

b. **Charitable trusts.** Like ILITs, charitable trusts used to be more common when more people had tax problems than do now. Charitable trusts come in several varieties, but the point is to put an asset that may have significant income or capital gains taxes attached into an irrevocable trust and direct its income, as an annuity stream, either to a charity or yourself, and then give the asset to the charity or yourself (whoever did not get the income stream). Doing this allows the creator of the trust to remove assets from his or her estate while also accomplishing a charitable goal.

c. **Medicaid asset protection trust.** A Medicaid Asset Protection Trust can give you a way to get assets out of your control so that you can qualify to have Medicaid cover long term care costs. As you know better than I do, paying for long term care is one of the biggest challenges facing our society over the next 30 years, as the baby boomer generation ages into Alzheimer's, dementia, and other expensive long term conditions. Meanwhile, you literally have to be down to almost your last dollar for Medicaid to take on these costs for you. If you have a client who may need Medicaid to cover long term care costs and wants to try to save assets for descendants, a Medicaid Trust may provide the answer. The challenge with Medicaid Trusts is that they do require the client to give up significant control over assets well before Medicaid is actually needed. Trying to put a Medicaid Trust in place after it has become apparent that the client is likely going to need care is like trying to buy homeowner's insurance after the house has caught on fire.

d. **Offshore asset protection trust.** As noted several times already, the beneficiaries of trusts set up for them by other people enjoy protection for the assets held by that trust. If a judgment gets entered against them, they can tell their creditor the assets in the trust are not theirs and are not available to pay it (it helps if, in addition to having the assets in the trust, the beneficiary is not the trustee, and if whoever is the trustee has full discretion as to whether and when to give trust assets to the beneficiary). In general, you cannot create a trust yourself, put your own assets into it, and then tell your creditors to buzz off. It is not impossible, however. It does take time, money, and administrative hassle to accomplish. For obvious reasons, the courts do not want to make it easy for people to evade their creditors. We also have the full faith and credit clause in the United States Constitution, requiring the various states to respect the judgments of the other states. And so moving money around from one jurisdiction to a different one with more friendly debtor laws does not necessarily create protection.

Enter offshore trusts. Although other countries are, obviously, not governed by the full faith and credit clause of the United States Constitution, many countries have treaties with the United States obligating them to cooperate with us in legal and tax matters (and vice versa). And so you cannot necessarily count on money outside of the country being protected from judgments or tax obligations here. There are, however, some jurisdictions, such as the Cook Islands, who have explicitly made it known that their justice system will not respect or enforce other countries' judgments. Money and other assets controlled by financial institutions there can be extremely difficult for creditors here to access.

When you hear the term "offshore trusts," you may be thinking to yourself that we are talking something that is really only for the ultra-wealthy. In fact, however, a person who is "ultra-wealthy" is probably the past point where they worry about losing a lawsuit. Determining where that line gets drawn is probably a personal decision, but the people who find sophisticated asset protection to be valuable may not be as rich as you would expect. The question is, how much does it take to make you interesting to potential litigants while not being so much that you could simply shrug off a judgement? I have seen people with six figure net worths find this top-level asset protection, which costs tens of thousands to set up and has significant ongoing maintenance costs, to be attractive.

e. **Domestic asset protection trust.** If asset protection sounds potentially interesting to your clients, but going offshore sounds too daunting, there are several states within the United States that have enacted statutory schemes that allow people to create self-settled asset protection trusts (*i.e.*, trusts that you can set up for yourself and of which you can be a beneficiary, but which supposedly will enjoy protection from your creditors). There are a number of steps that need to be followed to give these any chance of working. Most notably, they need to be set up will before creditor problems appear on the horizon. There is a statute of limitations that varies by state, but at the minimum, the trust needs to be in place and funded at least a couple of years before it will be respected. Second, the trustee of the trust needs to be in the state in which the trust is located, and it probably should be a professional. Third, the trust, of course needs to be irrevocable, and you do need to turn over control of the assets to the trustee (although the trustee will be managing those assets under the instructions you created).

Even with all these administrative hassles in place, because these trusts are, by definition, located domestically, the courts under which they are governed are subject to the full faith and credit clause of the United States Constitution. It seems, therefore, difficult to be sure they would hold up if challenged and, indeed, there are several examples of these kinds of trusts being "busted" and the assets inside being used to satisfy an adverse judgment. These types of trusts are still relatively new and the law around them is still nascent and developing.

5. **Special needs trust.** If you want to give money to someone who qualifies for government assistance due to low income, you need to proceed carefully. The danger is that you will give them enough money to disqualify them from receiving benefits, but not enough to actually cover their special needs. And the money that you do end up giving to them simply goes right through their hands to pay for services that would have been covered anyway by the benefits they now no longer qualify to receive.

To address this situation, you need to leave assets to people who may qualify for such benefits in a "special needs trust." A special needs trust prohibits the trustee from paying for items that can qualify for coverage by government programs. That may sound backwards ("My trustee won't be able to pay for my special needs kid's very expensive medical care?"). But placing that kind of restriction on how those funds can be spent keeps them available for other items that would not be covered by government benefits.

The requirements for setting up a special needs trust are specific and intricate, and go far beyond just limiting how the money can be spent. Even among attorneys who specialize in estate planning, special needs trust planning is more specialized still. If you have clients with this particular concern, you need to encourage them not only to get it done (assets passing to a special needs beneficiary via the intestate rules is a *total disaster*!), but to get it done by someone who knows this particular niche.

6. **Pet trust**. Does including your pets in your estate plan seem… indulgent? Like something only an "eccentric" cat lady would do? Not so fast! The death of an owner is a frequent cause of pets ending up in shelters. You know how much your pet costs. The food. The vet bills. The toys. The litter. The scratching posts. Etc., etc., etc. Setting up a trust for your pets is not necessarily about spoiling them. If you want to be sure that your pets will be cared for in a particular manner or by a particular person, setting aside the money for that purpose is the only way to ensure it will happen. Sure, you could just give the money, and the pets, to the person who you want to care for them. But if given the pets and the money outright, the recipient of those items does not have any legal obligation with regard to either one. They can drop the pet off at the shelter and then take that money to the mall for a shopping spree. If the money is, instead, being held by a trustee, that person is obligated to follow your instructions and not use the money for their own benefit.

A pet trust also gives you a way to direct what will happen to unspent funds. If you give money outright to someone for pet care, you may end up way overshooting on the amount needed, and the person now has an unexpected windfall. A trust lets you set aside more than you think will be needed and then direct who will get the remaining funds after your pet dies.

7. **Gun trust**. If you own firearms and are concerned about where they would go after your death, you need to proceed with caution (and if you are a personal representative or a trustee managing an estate or trust with firearms in then, you really need to proceed with caution). Depending on the type of firearm, there may be restrictions on who can receive them, steps that may need to be taken if they will cross state lines, and requirements for how that transfer needs to be recorded. Moreover, the upkeep and maintenance of guns can be rigorous and expensive. This can get so complicated, and the consequences for getting it wrong can be so serious, that special trusts have been created just for the purpose of holding and transferring guns. Whether such a trust makes sense for your client depends on the number of guns they have, the type, and how opinionated they are about where they would want those guns to end up.

Chapter 3
Why should your clients plan their estates?

Hopefully, at this point, I have made progress in convincing you that the number of estate planning situations that are simple are few and far between. But that news may not convince your clients that they need to plan their estates. In fact, it may make them want to bury their heads even deeper in the sand. The thing about estate planning is that, even if you do not sit down at least occasionally and consider how your affairs would be handled for you if you could not handle them yourself, somehow, someway, it would be figured out. The difficult part about convincing people to put some thought and money into their estate plan is that the person on whom the burden of a bad plan would fall most heavily is not the person who needs to, or even can, do the planning. The person who needs to do the planning would, by definition, be the one person blissfully unaware of the chaos potentially taking place.

So why make this time and money investment, and why do it now? I mean, this plan is probably not going to be needed tomorrow, right?

It's gonna to be needed at some point

Perhaps the strangest part about the reluctance to engage in estate planning is that it heavily involves the two things that are most notoriously inevitable, but about which people are most reluctant to think or confront: death and taxes. This is happening! You are going to die! And when you do, somebody is going to have to wrap up your affairs and disburse your stuff to someone else. Yet, a lot of people think this is wasted effort because it seems like death is probably a long way off. Maybe it is, but of course, very few of us can be sure.

If you plan to do anything other than leave money outright to adults, you literally have to document that desire

As explained earlier, there are rules for where your assets would go, even if you do not have a will. But those rules leave your assets outright to the people entitled to receive them. If those people are unable to manage money, because of age or disability, or should not manage money, because of immaturity, high liability professions or hobbies, or other, more serious challenges, such as drug addiction, simply leaving them even a seemingly modest amount of money outright will cause more problems than it solves, and the size of those problems could be significant. Imagine receiving a windfall right in the middle of a divorce. Or receiving an amount that is only enough to disqualify you from receiving Medicaid, but not enough to cover the life-preserving medical treatment you need to deal with a chronic medical condition. Or suddenly having access to 10 years' worth of salary to dedicate to an opioid addiction. If your beneficiaries are minor kids, you are shooting in the dark as to whether any of these or similar scenarios will be relevant. Leaving money to people who are or might be in these situations may result in your loving gift being a curse rather than a blessing. This is much more common than most people realize.

Low probability event, but potential disaster if it happens

Yes, you probably are not going to die or suffer a major incapacitating event anytime soon. But this is a classic "low probability, extreme negative consequence" event. That is, if you are wrong (and inevitably, someday, you will be wrong), the resulting consequences can be truly catastrophic for people who have to pick up the pieces. At some point, these consequences are bad enough that even though they are unlikely, it is still worth taking steps to address, mitigate, or avoid them.

But how low is the probability, especially for disability?

Before getting too glib about how unlikely an estate plan is to be needed, we should ask, how likely is it to be needed? The chance that it will be needed on any particular day is quite low, even for more elderly clients, which is what causes clients to feel as though they can safely put it off. Of course, eventually, everyone will need one. In between those extremes, there is a greater than zero chance that you will need it. Greater than most people would probably guess as a matter of fact:

Exact Age	Male Death Probability	Male Number of Lives	Male Life Expectancy	Female Death Probability	Female Number of Lives	Female Life Expectancy
30	0.001626	97,393	47.75	0.000740	98,588	51.95
31	0.001669	97,235	46.82	0.000792	98,515	50.99
32	0.001712	97,072	45.90	0.000841	98,437	50.03
33	0.001755	96,906	44.98	0.000886	98,354	49.07
34	0.001800	96,736	44.06	0.000929	98,267	48.11
35	0.001855	96,562	43.14	0.000977	98,175	47.16
36	0.001920	96,383	42.22	0.001034	98,080	46.20
37	0.001988	96,198	41.30	0.001098	97,978	45.25
38	0.002060	96,006	40.38	0.001171	97,870	44.30
39	0.002141	95,809	39.46	0.001253	97,756	43.35
40	0.002240	95,603	38.54	0.001347	97,633	42.41
41	0.002362	95,389	37.63	0.001452	97,502	41.46
42	0.002509	95,164	36.72	0.001571	97,360	40.52
43	0.002684	94,925	35.81	0.001706	97,207	39.59
44	0.002890	94,671	34.90	0.001857	97,041	38.65
45	0.003121	94,397	34.00	0.002022	96,861	37.72
46	0.003386	94,102	33.11	0.002204	96,665	36.80
47	0.003707	93,784	32.22	0.002411	96,452	35.88

Exact Age	Male Death Probability	Male Number of Lives	Male Life Expectancy	Female Death Probability	Female Number of Lives	Female Life Expectancy
48	0.004091	93,436	31.34	0.002648	96,220	34.96
49	0.004531	93,054	30.46	0.002910	95,965	34.06
50	0.005013	92,632	29.60	0.003193	95,686	33.15
51	0.005524	92,168	28.75	0.003491	95,380	32.26
52	0.006059	91,659	27.90	0.003801	95,047	31.37
53	0.006611	91,103	27.07	0.004119	94,686	30.49
54	0.007187	90,501	26.25	0.004449	94,296	29.61
55	0.007800	89,851	25.43	0.004813	93,877	28.74
56	0.008456	89,150	24.63	0.005201	93,425	27.88
57	0.009144	88,396	23.83	0.005583	92,939	27.02
58	0.009865	87,588	23.05	0.005952	92,420	26.17
59	0.010622	86,724	22.27	0.006325	91,870	25.32
60	0.011458	85,802	21.51	0.006749	91,289	24.48

Source: Social Security Actuarial Life Table, 2015, https://www.ssa.gov/oact/STATS/table4c6.html

Are you advising your clients to buy life and disability insurance?

The urgency of needing an estate plan is revealed by the urgency of needing disability and life insurance. You would never advise a client to start investing before confirming they at least had adequate life insurance, and probably disability insurance too. But if those insurance plans would send cash out into a void during an emergency, with no guidance about who should manage it or how, it could create at least as many problems as it solves. If that money is going to a child, for example, a conservator needs to be appointed by a court to manage the money for the child until he or she turns 21, at which point the money is theirs, ready or not.

Even if the money is going to a responsible adult, as explained earlier, windfalls are almost always difficult to resist spending and *usually* end up getting frittered away on short term splurges. Remember that filling out the designated beneficiary instructions on an insurance policy *is* estate planning, but only partially. The instructions about what to do with the funds after that have been distributed is the critical second half.

Getting the right people in charge

Perhaps the most important part of the plan is not the instructions, but the people appointed to carry them out. Even a really good, thorough plan will have a number of points at which someone has to step in and make a choice from a number of different options.

Sure, this house is part of the pot that is supposed to be divided equally between three kids, but does that mean we sell it, or distribute it to all three kids as co-owners? Or maybe distribute it to one kid while giving other parts of the estate to the other two. If we do that, who gets to decide the value of the various items being distributed out? If we are going to sell it, what is our goal? To sell it (and get cash) as fast as possible? Or to maximize the sale price? What about the stuff inside the house? Do we sell all of that or distribute it out to the heirs? What if two or more of those heirs claim to want the same things?

These are the kind of questions that require having a diligent person with high integrity and who everyone trusts running the show. Hoping that person finds their way to the position without any guidance from you is a recipe for disaster.

Leaving a legacy of organization (or, not letting your loved ones' last memory of you be about the mess you left for them)

In the best of circumstances, wrapping up someone's affairs after they have passed away can be difficult, time consuming work. Even if the decedent was an elderly person who had their documents in order, a funeral has to be planned, assets need to be identified, creditors need to be found, a last tax return needs to be filed, personal property needs to be distributed, given away, sold, or thrown out, real property needs to be cleaned up and sold or donated, etc., etc., etc.

Now, imagine if the death was not expected, and the needed documentation is not well organized or not up to date. Or, imagine that there are substantial creditor claims. Or, imagine that there is a non-cooperative heir in the mix. All things that happen all the time. Any one of these factors can make this already challenging task incredibly time consuming and difficult.

Financial and tax efficiency

At the time of this writing, the threshold at which the estate tax becomes an issue for people is so high – more than $11 million per individual, and more than $22 million per married couple – that almost no one has an estate tax problem anymore. But that does not mean people are not making serious tax mistakes as they transfer property among family members.

One of the most common mistakes people make is using lifetime transfer techniques to avoid probate, but then missing out on a huge capital gains tax avoidance. A common example of this is people putting their adult kids on the title to their real property. As explained earlier, yes, making your adult kids joint owners of your house will automatically make that house theirs when you die, but they will inherit that house with your capital gains basis, which could result in tens, or even hundreds, of thousands of dollars of capital gains tax that would have been avoided if the property had been transferred at death instead.

And then there is the efficiency of the transfer. How quickly would your clients' dependents and the people caring for them, such as guardians, need money? As noted earlier, I do not automatically advise everyone that they must avoid probate, but one reality of probate is that it frequently takes more than a year for creditor concerns to be fully put to rest and money to be distributed. If that seems potentially problematic, a fully funded living trust can provide more flexibility and quicker results.

Chapter 4
How can estate planning strengthen your relationship with your clients?

Many financial advisors that I encounter seem to understand that, yes, estate planning is important and is something their clients need to consider. But they seem to view it as something that is ancillary, or even external, to the service they are providing to their clients. This is a huge missed opportunity. Participating in your clients' estate planning, and really getting to understand how those plans work and why they were set up the way they were, can reveal significant needs and opportunities to address well beyond having an emergency cash fund on hand and saving for retirement.

Deeper understanding of your clients' needs and goals

Although most wealth advisors work hard to get a comprehensive understanding of their clients' financial picture, there are frequently at least three barriers to getting full disclosure.

First, especially at the beginning of the relationship, before trust has been developed, the client may want to hold at least a little back from you, just in case the relationship does not work out. Or maybe because they feel nervous about what they might see as a loss of control. Or maybe they are worried about the fees.

A conversation with an estate planning attorney, on the other hand, will come at this inquiry from a different angle. Unlike in a conversation with a financial advisor, in which the client may feel as though they can limit the information they are disclosing to just the assets with which they want assistance, a good estate planning process requires full disclosure from the clients. They should not have any incentive to hold back.

Second, the financial planning process is frequently focused on wealth accumulation or preservation for lifetime goals. A lot of financial planning literature does refer to "leaving a legacy" as being part of the conversation, but in my experience, that conversation focuses mostly on wealth accumulation or preservation as well, and not in the mechanics of how that legacy will be realized. A conversation about those mechanics can reveal more particulars about the client's goals and concerns.

Uncover additional financial needs

In many cases, our relationship with our clients is limited not just by what we think to ask them, but also what they think to ask us. Unfortunately, clients rarely know what is possible beyond our most basic offerings. Many potential clients come to me, for example, focused entirely on instructing how their assets should be distributed if they die. That obviously is an important part of estate planning, but completely ignores the large favor you can do for your heirs by holding their money for them in an asset-protected entity.

Similarly, on the financial planning side, I see many clients who do not appreciate some of the more creative savings options available to them via life insurance. They also tend to dramatically underestimate the amount of life insurance their family would truly need in their absence.

Coming at these issues from different angles frequently opens clients' eyes to ways that we can be helpful to them beyond just our most basic offerings.

Learn about family concerns that you can potentially address

Those of us who provide professional services can sometimes get so enamored with talking about the technical features and benefits of the services we are providing that it can be easy to miss talking about the underlying family dynamics that may be motivating the clients' top-level decisions. Sometimes these can be easy conversations to skip because they are uncomfortable. Sometimes the clients do not even realize the connection between the services they are buying and their underlying motivations for buying them.

The family dynamics, however, should be a foundational part of a comprehensive estate planning process. Again, we are coming at this from a different angle which can sometimes force conversations that would have a huge impact on the advice you are giving, but which the clients did not think (or did not want) to bring up.

Establish a relationship with future generations

As I understand it, one of the biggest problems financial advisors face is that, when the client dies, the people who inherit the client's assets almost always remove the assets from that advisor's custody. Involving yourself in your clients' estate planning can address this problem by opening up conversations between the financial advisor and the next generation, and if the client will allow you in, it can be a great way to plant the seeds of a relationship with the eventual recipients of those funds. Both the estate planner and the financial advisor can benefit greatly by facilitating these discussions.

Avoid getting sucked into a nasty family squabble after your client dies

As the custodians of money that is being fought over, financial advisors can often unwittingly find themselves in the middle of nasty family squabbles. Family members who are not the advisor's client and who have no legal right to know about or decide anything can decide that they are going to get their way by being difficult. Often, the advisor can deal with the situation by referring back to company policies and procedures that they do not control. But wouldn't it be nice to avoid the situation in the first place?

Maybe you can by encouraging your client to have the hard conversations about how this is going to work before a difficult situation arrives. So many people assume that their family is full of reasonable people who will figure it out. The number of estate situations that I see that range somewhere between uncomfortable and nasty suggests otherwise.

Chapter 5
Finding the right attorney to send your clients to

Is there anything scarier in business than making a referral? Especially to someone who has not performed a service for you personally? And especially to someone who does something in which you do not necessarily have substantial training yourself? What follows are some thoughts and guidance on what to look for when choosing an attorney to recommend to your clients.

Is an attorney necessary?

Perhaps before referring your clients to an attorney, you need to consider whether the assistance of an attorney is even necessary. Thanks to large, investor-backed companies running slick, national marketing campaigns, everyone knows that there are do-it-yourself options available for creating estate plans that are almost certainly going to be much cheaper than using an attorney. If asked directly, most people would probably agree that these quick, cheap, do-it-yourself options are going to be less sophisticated than an attorney-drafted plan. But hey, it's got to be better than nothing, right?

Wrong! A poorly thought out estate plan absolutely can be worse than nothing. I may not be a representative sample, but every contested probate matter in which I have been involved has had a will underlying it. But the decedent either failed to appreciate how the will fit in with his or her other planning components, such as property titling and designated beneficiary instructions. Or the decedent created situations that did not work for the family, especially co-ownership of non-cash-producing, hard-to-liquidate assets, such as remote vacation properties.

At the risk of sounding like a broken record, the other common mistake people make when trying to plan around something with which they have no experience and only superficial knowledge is failing to appreciate the importance of putting the right people into the various roles. Or to even understand what makes a good person for each role. These do-it-yourself options can certainly produce simple wills and trusts, but rarely provide the critical counseling that a good attorney will provide about how to ensure that the entire plan is cohesive and is being run by the right people.

Attorney qualities to consider

Just about every attorney thinks they can draft a will, and a lot of small firms list estate planning among the services they provide, even when the other services (such as DUI defense, bankruptcy, family law, etc.) may not seem to have much overlap with estate planning. In a sense, these attorneys are right. Anyone can draft a will. I see many attorney-drafted wills that are not any more sophisticated than simple wills that can be bought on line for less than $200. Unlike some other areas of law, like medical malpractice litigation or mergers and acquisitions, where even the most straightforward cases are complex and take significant resources just to get started, estate planning lends itself to dabbling. Just as with lay people, attorneys with little to no relevant experience can find a form, fill in the blanks, and say they created an estate plan.

But also just like a layperson, an attorney who is dabbling is going to fail to appreciate the nuances inherent in most estate planning situations. In fact, the simpler the situation appears, the more likely it is that the seeming simplicity is the result of not knowing what they are missing instead of it actually being simple (see the Wikipedia entry for "the Dunn-Krueger Effect" for more on this phenomenon).

Estate planning pulls in many different areas of law and combines with a subtle knowledge of human psychology. It is a true area of specialty, and sending your clients to someone who sees estate planning as a sideshow is a mistake. You may feel the same way about competitors who primarily specialize in taxes or who sell insurance and also claim to be able to advise on investing. Each one of those topics require too much knowledge to be able to do all of them well.

Financial success does not equal quality attorney

This probably is not limited to the practice of law, and I am sure you see it in your own industry, but the best businesspeople, and especially the best marketers, are not necessarily the best lawyers. I am certain that if you asked your clients to name some lawyers that they have heard of and then took a survey of lawyers about who their most impressive colleagues are, there would be no overlap.

On one hand, you may want certain outer confirmations of success and competence. The range of possibilities in the estate planning world is wide, from attorneys who truly are "solos" and hold client meetings in coffee shops to people in Class A downtown office space with a small army of associates, paralegals, and assistants. My suggestion would be that the attorney to whom you refer your clients should have a similar office setting and employee structure as you do. You know your clients are comfortable with that. If your clients are used to dealing with you directly and you maintain a casual atmosphere, the coffee shop lawyer might be the right choice.

Rapport with you

Although we all want the people to whom we refer our clients to have a certain level of social skill and be able to impress our clients, judging your referral sources on how they bond with you can be a misleading metric. If you have hired an employee, you may be familiar with the challenge here. It can be easy to fall in love with the person who interviews best, but the ability to wow someone for an hour and the ability to competently perform a job that will inevitably have periods of stress, boredom, and difficulty over a long period of time are two different qualities.

All things being equal, sure, send your clients to the attorney you like best. But when you personally bond well with one particular attorney, you may actually want to raise your guard up higher and ask whether you are sure you are evaluating this person based on the right criteria. The fact that you grew up in the same area of the country or root for the same football team is not a great reason to make a referral, but subconsciously, it may be having a huge impact over how you feel about the person.

Rapport with clients

Your clients' rapport with the attorney to whom you send them is probably more important than your rapport with the attorney because really, the extent to which they enjoy their time with the attorney will serve as a large determinant with regard to how they end up feeling about the experience. The reality is that, as much effort as the attorney should put into educating your clients about how their plans work, this is inherently complicated stuff that the attorney has spent years studying at a very high level. We usually cannot convey the meaning and reasoning behind every part of the plan in the amount of time that most clients want to spend talking to us about it.

Because of the complexity of the underlying product, clients are going to rely heavily on other parts of the experience to determine whether they feel good or bad about how it went, and their general feelings of warmth (or not) towards the attorney, and the feeling that he or she really understood their concerns, will play an outsized role in their final assessment of how satisfied they are with the end product.

There is not one attorney who can achieve good rapport with everyone. As with considerations about the attorney's office setting discussed above, different attorneys will likely have an easier time establishing rapport with some clients with others, and that probably should be a part of your calculus when deciding to whom to refer.

Should the attorney to whom you refer specialize in estate planning?

As noted earlier, there is something about estate planning that makes just about anyone think they can do it. And the fact is that, really, anyone *can* put together an estate plan. Putting together a *good* estate plan is almost always challenging, but if you are capable of writing a document that contains your wishes and signing that document in front of two people, you are capable of drafting a will.

If laypeople think they are up to the task of drafting an estate plan, you can only imagine what attorneys think they can do, even if their real area of specialty is in something entirely different. But an attorney who does not specialize in estate planning may not have any knowledge about it beyond what a layperson has. This area of law is so broad and so nuanced that no person can know everything. And in fact, estate planning might be one of the more complicated areas of law because it touches on so many different topics. There is the nuts and bolts of passing property from one person to another, of course. But then there is also tax law, marital planning, family dynamics, business law, insurance law, and many more complicated topics. A lawyer who does not engage in and study estate planning all the time is just as susceptible as a layperson to overlooking the complexity underlying every person's plan. If it seems simple, maybe that is because it is. Or it might seem simple because you are so clueless that you do not know where the landmines and potholes are.

Credentials

Your clients do not care about credentials. As someone who went to the second most expensive law school in the country, in large part because of its prestigious reputation, it pains me to admit this. But it would surprise me to find out I have been asked which school I attended by even five prospective clients. And I am not sure whether any of the prospective clients who did ask became actual clients.

The one credential that might matter to your clients is the length of time the attorney has been practicing, and especially how long they have been focusing on estate planning law. Most people do not want to be someone's first client (although every one of us had to have one of those), but before you send your clients to the most experienced attorney you can find, be aware that a lot of clients want an attorney who is younger than them. Most clients do realize that this is something they may have to revisit several times over the course of their lives, and they take reassurance that this person will be in it with them through the long haul. The number of clients I have had come to me update a plan that was drafted by an attorney who has since retired is growing all the time.

Office setting

Office setting may seem unimportant, but actually can make a big, if subconscious, difference in the minds of your clients. I highly recommend visiting the offices of the people to whom you refer. Your gut instinct may be that a nicer office is better than one that is not as nice, but I suggest that the best match for you and your clients is going to be one that is similar to yours. In other words, if you are in a retail location with ground level access, you need to consider whether your clients will be comfortable driving downtown, parking in a garage, and riding an elevator up 30 floors. That office is likely gorgeous, but also may send off signals of exclusivity with which your clients may feel uncomfortable.

On the other side of the spectrum, your clients who are used to dealing with a professional in a traditional office setting may feel put off by meeting with an attorney in a space that is obviously temporary, or even less formal, such as a coffee shop or library.

Different clients will have different expectations and levels of comfort with different settings, and every type of arrangement can work for someone. But the safest way for you to proceed is to find an arrangement and atmosphere with which you already know your clients are familiar and comfortable.

Staff

There is a popular misconception about small businesses of all types – that a business with few, or no, employees is more efficient, and therefore cheaper than one with lots of staff. While it is true that a business with few employees can (or maybe has to) provide a more personal touch, if the owner is doing everything, he or she has to overcharge for parts of the process in order to stay afloat. While most clients want to be able to get their lawyer on the phone without having to go through layers of staff who may or may not be familiar with their particular situations, most people probably do not want to pay their lawyer to set up the conference room, make the coffee, print and organize documents, or run to the office supply store to pick up paper. It might not be a determinative factor on its own, but you probably want to find a sweet spot between an inefficient or impersonal bureaucracy and an attorney who is quite literally a solo practitioner.

Process

One point that probably should not be negotiable with the attorneys to whom you are referring is whether they have a consistent process that they use for every client. One thing that can be sure to drive clients nuts in every customer service setting is not knowing what to expect. It is why franchise restaurants tend to succeed so much more often than individual restaurants. People will choose predictability in service and food quality over the possibility of getting a better product or price.

This desire for a predictable product is probably even more pronounced when it comes to something that is as mysterious to most people as legal assistance. You do not necessarily need to be able to explain to your clients what the attorney's process is, but it will be substantially more likely that your clients will report a good experience back to you if you feel certain that the attorney does have a process that he or she consistently follows.

To be clear, this does not mean that every client should get the same end product. I sometimes joke that being a good lawyer depends on your ability to plagiarize. At its heart, the practice of law is about taking decisions that have worked previously and applying them to new situations. You would not want your lawyer turning on their computer and starting with a blank page.

On the other hand, maybe more than any other area of law, estate planning lends itself to copying and pasting, and sticking everyone into the same general plan without much customization. There is a balance between giving everyone a predictable process and being impersonal. Some lawyers are better at finding that balance than others. You will probably hear from your clients of the attorney to whom you send them is too far on one side or the other.

Pricing

Perhaps the most difficult variable to assess when it comes to estate planning is also the most obvious: price. As you are probably well aware, deciding what to charge for an intangible service, and communicating the value of that service to potential clients, presents a challenge that is nowhere near as difficult for tangible goods. When comparing cars, for example, even for people who know little about cars, it is easy to see that, yes, this more expensive car has more features than the cheaper one.

But what makes one estate plan better than another, and maybe worth paying more for? And even if one plan is objectively better than another, do your clients need the best plan available? To return to my car analogy, is there an estate planning equivalent to the car that gets you from point A to point B? A plan that is good enough to meet your basic needs, even if it does not have all the available bells and whistles?

Unfortunately, there is not any way to say what an estate plan should cost. There are so many factors that can affect it, not least of which is your clients' subjective measure of value. But, it is very difficult to put together an estate plan without some significant personal time with the client and if an attorney is charging an amount that would not seem to enable them to do that, you may want to inquire further about the amount of personal attention your clients can expect. In my experience, clients who hire an attorney expect a certain amount of interaction with that attorney and some assurance that they are receiving personal attention, not just being shuffled through an assembly line process and given standardized documents. Providing that assurance does require charging a sustainable amount of fees. In all likelihood, that fee is going to be more than your smallest clients can afford.

Ability to refer back

One question I frequently receive from potential new referral sources is whether, in exchange for receiving referrals, I will refer clients back. To be frank, this question is a strong indication to me that this budding relationship is unlikely to work out. I also hear complaints from people who ask this question that attorneys do not refer back. There are several reasons for why attorneys have this reputation.

First, most estate planning practices are built on referrals. When you refer your clients to an attorney, you want to know that the attorney is not going to suggest one of your competitors to that client. And so if most clients are coming from referrals, even a thriving practice may have fewer opportunities to refer than you would expect.

Second, an estate planning attorney's relationship with his or her clients is very different from the typical relationships a financial advisor has with his or her clients. Every estate planning attorney aspires to enter that ring of "trusted advisors" in their clients' minds. But, despite our best efforts, most clients view their relationship with their estate planning attorney as a one-time transaction. This is because the attorney is viewed by most clients as money spent to avoid loss. It is like a life insurance bill. It is critical to have insurance, but it is not a fun bill to pay. Your services, on the other hand, are resulting in gains for your clients. That is a little easier to swallow. Moreover, most financial advisors are able to bill their clients in a way that does not require them to take out their checkbooks and write checks.

Third, the number of new clients an estate planning attorney needs to sustain his or her practice is significantly higher than the typical financial advisor who receives ongoing payment from long-term clients. There are going to be natural limits on the number of clients that even an extremely busy financial advisor can refer to an estate planning attorney. This structural incongruity between a financial advisor's business model and an estate planning attorney's almost guarantees an imbalance in referrals between the advisor and the attorney because the attorney needs so many more new clients than the typical financial advisor. This means that the attorney has a lot more financial advisors to keep happy than the other way around. The math does not allow an attorney to keep every referral source happy with an equal number of reciprocal referrals.

Licensing and insurance

You may assume that the attorney to whom you are considering referring clients is properly licensed and insured, but that could be a huge mistake, especially because this information is usually publicly available and easy to check. The level of professional liability insurance, especially, can vary widely between attorneys. In Colorado, attorneys are not required to carry it. As a former plaintiff-side attorney, I can assure you that, when things go wrong and a lawsuit needs to be filed, you look for every possible pocket you can find for compensation. If the attorney does not have the ability to cover for a mistake, the professional who sent them there could certainly find themselves on the hook. It probably also is not a bad idea to confirm that they have other insurance, such as business insurance to deal with situations, such as clients injuring themselves in the parking lot.

Beyond the practical considerations of confirming that your referral partner is adequately insured, this could give you valuable insight into their aptitude for the work. At its heart, the practice of law, especially estate planning law, is the identification and mitigation of risk. If the attorney has not taken even the most basic, obvious step to protect themselves and their clients, it probably should raise questions about their ability to see much more subtle risks for which their clients' plans should account.

Chapter 6
Your role in the process

Is there any benefit to you of being more involved in the planning process beyond just making the referral? That is a trick question designed to see if you were paying attention. Again, your job unavoidably requires you to make estate planning decisions with your clients, whether you explicitly refer to it as estate planning and whether you encourage your clients to speak to an attorney. Remember that titling accounts and designating beneficiaries comes in front of the documents an attorney will draft for your clients during the estate distribution process. But even after you get an attorney involved, there are lots of opportunities for you to find and add value for your clients.

Identify the clients who need planning help

Those of us in the estate planning world, of course, think that everyone needs an estate plan. And we're right! As noted above, some of the people who may think they need it the least (single, childless adults with modest assets) may need it the most (who is going to speak for those people in an incapacity situation?). But admittedly, some need it more than others. And you are in a good spot to help those people identify themselves and motivate them to take action.

Probably the most important trigger to needing an estate plan is when you have someone relying on you. The most common situation where this becomes an issue is when kids enter the picture, but it can also happen at marriage or when an elderly parent needs more help than before. When you see dependents being given ownership interests in significant assets (the most common scenario involving minor kids is UTMA accounts, although sometimes we see kids being added to the house title) or being named as direct beneficiaries of life insurance policies and retirement accounts, that is a sign that is time to have a discussion about what would actually happen if something unexpected came to pass.

Attend the planning meeting?

Most estate planning attorneys will have at least two meetings with their clients to plan, if not three or four. One of those meetings is usually designated as the "planning meeting," at which the client's needs and concerns are probed, and the appropriate plan is developed. The lawyer may invite you to attend this meeting. In my experience, the vast majority of financial advisors turn that invitation down. You may, however, want to consider attending that meeting for at least a few reasons.

First, it can deepen your relationship with your clients. Of course, a client's family dynamics are going to influence how they handle their finances, and they should be talking about those issues with you anyway. But I find that clients frequently fail to consciously make that connection between the financial decisions they are making and their family relationships. Even if they do make that connection, the estate planning conversation is going to come at these issues from a different angle, and will frequently reveal issues and concerns that simply would not come up in other contexts. These issues and concerns frequently provide insight into the most intimate parts of a client's life. Being part of that conversation may deepen your bond with your client and provide ideas for how you can service your clients that may not have otherwise been apparent to you.

Second, your role in effectuating the estate plan before and after the lawyer does his or her work is at least as important as what the lawyer does, and you need to know what the plan is. When a lawyer creates an estate plan, the client frequently comes away from it with the misunderstanding that the documents are the plan. For the documents to work as intended, however, the client often must revisit asset titling decisions made before the documents were created, and then continue to remember and coordinate future titling decisions with the plan. You were likely a critical part of the before decisions, and will continue to be a critical part of the after decisions.

Third, the planning process frequently unveils additional needs, especially for emergency liquidity. One of the biggest challenges in administering an estate can arise when there are valuable assets, but little to no liquidity. The most common example is an estate in which the primary asset is real estate. Real estate can be challenging because, not only can it be difficult and time consuming to sell, but it can be expensive to maintain and insure until it is sold. Disagreements can readily break out about how quickly it should be sold, how much prep work should be done to get it ready for sale, and what upkeep and maintenance should be performed while waiting for it sell. These problems can be a lot easier to figure out if the estate contains sufficient cash to handle these challenges without outside support, and even make a partial distribution while the beneficiaries wait for the estate to be finalized. But having that cash takes planning and that is, obviously, where you come in.

Funding

Just as important as creating the documents that describe the plan is coordinating the asset titling and beneficiary designation instructions with that plan. The number of people who fail to correctly complete this step is distressingly high. Your will or trust only controls what is pointed at or contained in it and many people's asset titling and designated beneficiary instructions are, intentionally or not, set up to circumvent their will or trust. It makes sense because, often times, these decisions were made before the will or trust was put into place.

Frequently, the lawyer who puts together the plan can assist with retitling real estate, but we are relying on the custodians of the other assets to assist with retitling those. Given that this is just as important as creating the plan in the first place, your knowledgeable assistance with this process can be a huge value add for your clients. It can also increase your clients' loyalty towards you because your knowledge and understanding of this part of their lives can make you uniquely indispensable, not just to them, but to the people relying on them as well. In other words, truly understanding your clients' estate planning goals can give you a way to connect with the people who will be receiving this money next and potentially encourage them to keep it under your management.

Being aware of the need to update

As noted earlier, clients fail to appreciate the ongoing nature of estate planning, thinking of it as a one-time event that they check off the list and maybe revisit in another decade or two. The reality is that people are continuously making decisions that will impact who would receive or be able to manage assets for them if they could not do it, in the event of their deaths but also during times of temporary incapacity.

As a person who is likely to be updated on these types of decisions and events – such as marriages, divorces, births, deaths, new financial accounts, new insurance policies, etc. – you can continuously remind clients how important it is to keep all these things up to date and working together. Again, that conversation will come up naturally for you as you update account ownership and designated beneficiary instructions. And again, your clients likely fail to appreciate how often they are making decisions that will, someday, dramatically affect their loved one's lives. You have a unique role that you can play to keep them on track. I hope you will use it.

Conclusion

The takeaway messages from this book are:

1. Estate planning is not a one-time event, but an ongoing process in which all of us are continuously engaged, whether we want to be or not.
2. As a financial advisor, you are on the front lines of the estate planning process, directly dealing with asset titling and beneficiary designations, both of which determine what impact a client's will or trust will have on the distribution of his or her estate.
3. Your proactive participation in the estate planning process can add significant value to your service offerings and deepen your relationships with your clients.

Whether your clients already view you as a "trusted advisor" or whether you are working to fill that role in their lives, understanding and becoming involved in their estate plans offers you a way to differentiate yourself from the crowd. Most advisors view estate planning as an ancillary to the important tasks, but estate planning is infused into everything you are doing with your clients. The more aware of and explicit about that you can become, the more value you can add for your clients, and the more indispensable you can become to them.

Next Steps

Now that your appreciation for the importance of estate planning and your role in getting it done has increased, you may be wondering where to go from here. A good estate planning attorney should be a foundational part of your professional network. If you are in the Denver area, we hope you will consider contracting us. You can call us at 303.578.2745, or visit our website at themckenziefirm.com.

[Appendix] Estate plan checkup

The following questions will help your clients determine if their current estate plan will accomplish the goals of providing for their care during incapacity, protecting their loved ones, and passing their assets to whom they want, when they want, and in the way they want. Any client who cannot confidently answer "yes" to all these questions should consider speaking with an estate planning professional about an update.

1.	Do you have a properly executed will or trust in place?
2.	Do you have a current Durable Power of Attorney?
3.	Do you have a current Health Care Power of Attorney?
4.	Do you have an Advanced Healthcare Directive (a.k.a. Living Will)?
5.	Has your current plan been reviewed in the last three years?
6.	Does your current plan contain a customized plan to determine if you are mentally disabled?
7.	Does your current plan give instructions for your care and the care of your loved ones in the event of your disability?
8.	Are you certain your current plan will minimize possible federal estate taxes at your death, including taxes on your house, life insurance, and IRAs?
9.	If you have a revocable trust, is it fully funded so that none of your assets will have to go through probate?

10. Have you taken steps to avoid possible will contests and disputes during the administration of your estate?
11. Does your current plan protect your children's inheritance:
a. From their own bad decisions?
b. In the event your spouse chooses to remarry?
c. From divorce, lawsuits, or other creditors?
12. Does your current plan protect assets passed to your surviving spouse:
a. In the event your surviving spouse chooses to remarry?
b. From creditors?
c. From lawsuits?
13. Have you recently checked the beneficiary designations of your retirement plans and life insurance policies?
14. Are you confident that you have not listed your estate or any minor children as either primary or secondary beneficiaries of your retirement plans and life insurance policies?
15. Does your current plan name guardians for your minor children?
16. Are you confident your current plan is income tax efficient?
17. Does your current plan name an executor or successor trustee?
18. Are you confident your executor, power of attorney, and successor trustee are prepared to act on your behalf when asked to?

[Appendix] Myths. Facts, and FAQs

As you probably encounter in your work with clients, most people have conceptions about estate planning based on myth and rumor that are sometimes not just wrong, but are the opposite of the truth. The following are some of the most common misconceptions that I encounter.

Myth: Avoiding probate is a must

In some states, the consensus is that avoiding probate is a must. But a number of states have vastly improved and simplified their probate processes, with options available to minimize court involvement and keep things moving along at a reasonable pace. Moreover, even if you do avoid probate, wrapping up someone's life always requires a certain amount of expense and hassle, whether it is done with court oversight or privately. And so, no, I do not automatically assume everyone should avoid probate in all cases.

Myth: Probate is for people who don't have a will

Lots of people are under the misunderstanding that having a will avoids probate. In fact, however, confirming the existence and validity of a will, giving any parties that have been negatively impacted by the instructions in the will a chance to object to it, and ensuring that the instructions in the will get properly followed are some of the primary purposes of the probate process. The need for probate is determined by the type, location, and amount of property that you own, not by the existence, or lack thereof, of a will.

Myth: Not having a plan is okay because the state has a default plan

The state does have a default plan that might match what you want, <u>if</u> <u>you die</u>. There is no default plan, however, for situations where you need help managing your affairs even though you are alive (*e.g.,* incapacity). And these situations are more common than most people think. If you end up in a situation where you need someone to manage your healthcare or finances (even temporarily) due to a significant injury or other medical development, a court has to conduct a very invasive analysis to confirm that you really need the help and that the person applying for the job is the right person to do it. This requires a case-by-case analysis that is usually expensive and grueling. Even people who are single, childless, and have only modest assets (or maybe, *especially* these people) need to think through this scenario and document their wishes in a legally enforceable way.

Myth: People only fight about money

Money can certainly bring out the worst in people, and sometimes, it can be truly surprising to find out how bad "the worst" can be. But there are so many subjects covered by a comprehensive estate plan that are ripe for extreme conflict in a situation that will be emotionally fraught anyway. Although it is hard to be certain because most family fights do not end up in court, and even if they did, there is no centralized database of what those fights are about, post-death asset distribution probably is the most common fodder for fighting. But fights about medical treatment decisions, money management during lifetime, end of life medical care, and memorial options can easily become throw down, relationship-ending battles among family members.

Also, money itself is easy to divide, even (or especially) when there is a lot of it. The smaller stuff (*i.e.,* the personal possessions) that may have little to no market value but significant sentimental value can become the subject of epic family brawls.

Myth: People only fight about unequal asset distributions

If your client thinks their family will not fight with one another because all they are doing is dividing everything up equally anyway, they may have another thing coming. Even when the instruction is to divide everything equally, there can still be a lot of decisions to make about what equal means. Is this piece of real estate equal to this other piece of real estate? Is this amount of cash fair compensation for this lamp that has no market value but significant sentimental value? Is an ownership interest in the family business equal to this amount of cash? The list can go on and on.

Second, the process of administering the estate can become a point of conflict. A common situation is one in which the kids are in significantly different financial situations, and one may need his or her distribution much more urgently than the others. And many times, the kid who is in the better financial situation is perceived to be the "responsible one" by the parents and is put in charge of everything as the trustee and personal representative. This can naturally lead to situations where the kids have strong disagreements with one another about how quickly the administration process can or should be carried out. One kid wants their money, *now*! The other kid wants to proceed very deliberately and cautiously to ensure they do not do anything that is going to get them sued.

Third, equal may seem unfair when one of the kids was providing more help to or getting more help from mom and dad during their lifetimes. A very common point of conflict is one in which one of the kids was living with the parents during the lifetimes rent free and the siblings feel as though they have already been given enough (or maybe even owe back rent to the estate). Another common point of conflict is one in which one of the kids provided significantly more care to the parents in their declining years than the other kids and feel as though they deserve compensation for that sacrifice. Frequently, both of these scenarios are present in the same case.

Myth: Creating documents is all you need to do

A lot of people sign their will or trust, breathe a sigh of relief, and check "estate planning" off the "to do" list. But it is absolutely critical that everyone understand that their asset titling and designated beneficiary instructions need to be revisited periodically to ensure they remain consistent with what the client wants to accomplish. And what the client wants to accomplish will almost certainly evolve over time as their assets change, and their kids age, and family members get married or divorced, or are born or die. As I tell my clients, this is never really over until it is really over, if you know what I am saying.

Myth: I can decide how complicated my estate plan needs to be

Most of my clients tell me that one of their priorities is to keep things simple. My first question, when I hear that plea, is, "Simple for who?" Remember, there are three people involved in every plan: the person making the plan, the person who will have to administer it, and the person who will receive its benefits. What is simple for one of those parties may result in complexity for the others. A simple plan to create may leave lots of difficult questions unanswered for the people who have to administer it.

The other thing to keep in mind is that many decisions will have already been made, and will continue to be made, that will influence how difficult the plan needs to be. If you are single and childless, and most of your assets are highly liquid, then sure, a short will and some beneficiary instructions can do the trick. But I frequently get asked to keep things simple by people who have step kids, lots of real estate, immature beneficiaries, etc. Sorry, but a short will that just says, "Give everything to my spouse if she survives me and split everything equally between my kids if she doesn't" is going to create so many more problems than it solves.

Myth: Putting my adult kids on my assets makes transfer easy

One surprisingly popular estate planning technique is adding adult kids (and sometime even minor kids) to the ownership of major assets. Putting them on the house, for, instance, or the financial accounts. There are some real pros to doing this. It results in an immediate transfer of the asset to those co-owners upon death. It also enables some management of the asset during periods of incapacity (although selling the asset without the full participation of all owners may still be impossible, absent a power of attorney or a court order).

In my opinion, however, these pros are almost always outweighed by significant cons. The two big ones are loss of step up in capital gains basis at death and opening yourself up to the liabilities of your new co-owners. Gifts received at death are taken at the value at the time of death. Gifts received during lifetime come with the donor's basis. This can result in tens of thousands of dollars of tax that could have been avoided.

And of course, with more owners come more potential creditors. Every person who gets added to an asset as an owner brings potential liabilities for which the asset could be eventually be on the line. When this possibility is brought to their attention, most people conclude that the idea of potentially listing their house as an asset in their son's divorce is not appealing.

Index